Startup Business Guide For Beginners:

Manual on How to Start and Build an Awesome Company, Find Business Partners and Invest in Startups

By

Dale Blake

Table of Contents

Startup Business Guide For Beginners: Manual on How to Start and Build an Awesome Company, Find Business Partners and Invest in Startups

By Dale Blake

Introduction

Earning a source of income is vital for every person, no matter who this person is. You can be the richest person in the world and still you'd have to have an income coming your way, as with money comes unlimited wants and in order to be able to fulfill these wants you constantly have to have money and since money is always limited you need to keep on earning more and more. And if you aren't super rich, then you definitely need to have an earning to be able to have the necessities of life.

So how does one earn money? There are two ways. You can either have a job in which you are working under someone and earning a constant salary under a contract. Other than that you can have your own business, where you are your own boss and can provide either items for sale or some sort of services. Being self employed and having your own business are sort of the same, with slight differences which will be explained later, but majorly being self employed also comes under having your own business. Some people prefer being on a job rather than having their own business but for others the case is opposite. Both categories have their advantages and disadvantages and what matters the most is what suits you. But for now we will be discussing on business and then on how to startup your own business.

Chapter 1. Business Basics

Before we move on to the discussion of how to startup your own business, we first need to discuss what actually a business is and the dynamics behind it.

What is a business?

People constantly need things whether it is for their survival, be it clothes, food or so on, or whether it is luxury items such as handbags, shoes and so on. So where do all these items come from? Obviously someone is making them or has set up a production facility that makes these items and distributes them to different areas from where retailers can go and buy them to put them up for sale in their stores, where the consumer can come and buy. So whoever is the backbone behind this process and is producing the items is running a business and is known as a businessman. So in simpler words, this whole economic activity described above is another name for a business.

Basically business is a manufacturing or sale/purchase of goods with the intention to earn profit from it.

And this profit that the businessman earns, is his source of income that we talked about earlier in the intro section.

Characteristics of any Business

- Exchange of goods/services: Any business will always involve the exchange of either certain goods or a specific service in return for money.

- Multiple transactions: Because the business owner is dealing with multiple people day in and day out and as a result they will be a part of numerous transactions on a daily basis.

- The target is Profit: The main goal of a business owner is to gain profit after providing his goods or services, as this is his source of income.

- Special Business Skills: Running a business is not every person's cup of tea and nor does everyone have the mental patience for it and as a result to be a successful business man you require special skills and an unmatched hunger for success.

- Different types of Risk: In the running of a business, any business owner must be aware that there are multiple risks that he will be taking due to which losses might occur. Some risks such as theft and fire or natural disasters can be insured against so the losses can be kept to a minimum but other risks such as different factors like changing demand or tastes are risk factors which can not insured against.

- Seller and Buyer: Any business mainly involves 2 parties, a buyer and a seller. Sometimes a middle man in the form of an agent might be there as well, but when looking at the bigger picture he will either be the buyer or seller or in certain situations both. And a business is a contract between these two parties.

- Industrial or commercial activity: Depending on what your business is producing it will come under either industrial activity or commercial activity. In the former category there is production of goods or services, while the latter is concerned with the marketing and distribution of goods and services.

- Consumer goods and producer goods: Business's deal with goods, which are of two types. Consumer goods are those which when bought can be directly consumed or used by the customer e.g. hair dryer, shampoo and so on. Producer goods on the other hand are those products that are used to further produce goods and these include equipment and machinery.

- Social responsibility: Business owners like any other individual have a social responsibility as well which means that they to need to make sure that the running of their business is in no way negatively affecting the environment or disturbing the people in the surrounding area. This is actually an important factor as these days many people prefer to buy goods and services from business's that are socially responsible as well as environmentally friendly.

A Business Vs. Self- Employment

Usually both of these terms are used interchangeably and while that too in general terms is correct as when you have your own business technically you are self-employed. But when you take a deeper look on a larger scale then you will see that there is a slight difference between the two. Self - employment is when you have your own thing going and you are the one who does most of the work and without you the functioning would stop, so basically it's a business but on a smaller scale. A business on the other hand is larger and as a result you have other people running it for you and even if you are not present, still your business operations can run smoothly. But since this is a startup business guide and since people usually start with small businesses, in this book we will be using the words business and self- employment interchangeably.

A Business or Job?

Different people have different views about whether they should have their own business or whether they should have a job. There is no right or wrong and you should do whatever you think is right for you. Both have their own set of advantages and disadvantages but the biggest advantage of your own business is that you are your own boss and you don't have to take any orders from someone else. So basically all the major decisions are in your hands and you can run the business the way you want and when and where you want, meaning you have lots of freedom. Having said that the biggest disadvantage of a business is that all the major workload and pressure is on you and you have to spend lots of time and money to set up your business and then get it going. Apart from that there is no job security and does involve some risks. But even after knowing these factors, still many people opt to have their own business as it gives them great satisfaction knowing that they are their own boss.

Chapter 2. Starting a Business

Being your own boss does have its perks, but that too means lots and lots of work and commitment to actually start and set up a business and then get it running smoothly. So now let's look at what is required to do all this.

For starters, the most important thing is that you need the mental commitment as well as an undeterred passion to succeed. Failure should not be an option. This is vital as many people each year try to set up their own businesses but due to a lack of mental strength and patience they either end up failing or they just give up too quickly as they do not have the patience to let their business run its initial course before it can start generating an income.

Setting up a business

To be able to set up a business, you must first know what good or service you want to or will be providing. But remember it can't be something out of the blue, it has to be something for which there is a demand or need for. Otherwise it is very unlikely your business will succeed. Because think about it, if you set up a business for which there is no demand, why would people want it, and if there is no buying then there are no profits and then you are likely to fail and no one wants that. So try to think of something for which there is a demand but add your own flair to it so that it becomes your own personal innovative thing and stands out from the rest.

Once you have an idea of what sort of business you want to set up, look at who your target audience will be. After identifying your target audience, try to mold your business and what it is providing according to the needs and taste of your target audience, so you know it will be popular among them and that they will end up buying it.

Business Plan

A business plan is basically a blue print or an outline for your business and its future. It is a document that contains what your business is about, your vision, the objectives you want to achieve and the strategies you will use to achieve them, your target market and the financial forecasts. So it is a great way to start up and plan your business as once you get down to making your business plan, everything about it will start to become clearer to you as well.

Business Plan Format

Though there are no set rules as to what has to be in your business plan and how long it should be, but it is always good to have a professional template to follow as that will give your business plan a formal touch and will help you in professional dealings where you have to show your business plans. A good business plan makes you look great as well. It gives off the impression that you are focused and well prepared to set up your own business and will help you close deals which are related to your business.

So here is a typical format for a business plan:

- Vision Statement: A short, comprehensive outline of the goals and the objectives of your business.

- The People: Highlight your strengths and write how you will be running the business and how you would try to overcome any problems that might occur. Also mention if you will be hiring some other people to help you and what the criteria for that would be.

- Business Profile: This is an important part of your business plan as in this part you will write and discuss what your business is actually about and what you will be doing and you are planning to go about running your business.

- Economic Assessment: In this section we explain the financial sides of your business and in what type of economic conditions you are setting it up. Also try to set up a cash flow assessment for 1 year, estimating where you will be spending money and where you will be generating money from. Apart from that make sure that you mention any risks you might face and how you are protecting yourself from it.

Importance of a Business Plan

A business plan is not only important for you, as it will help you gather an insight into your business and you will be able to collect all your thoughts in relation to your business and then put them in a picture so that it becomes clearer to you and so that you are better able to identify your business's strengths and weaknesses. Apart from that, it is also important, as it will help you secure financial funding or loans from any bank or financial institutions. Other than that it will help you get sponsors, make dealings with vendors and most

importantly if you need to get any partners, it will help

you get one.

Chapter 3. Business Structures

Choosing a business structure is one of the most important decision any entrepreneur can make before establishing their business as the type of business structure will help determine what tax bracket you will fall in and thus what amount of tax you should pay on the income of the business. Also the business structure you choose determines what paperwork and legal documents you have to fill. Without licenses and legal documentation, no potential business can be recognized in the business market as an enterprise.

 Personal liability is any form of debt taken upon by the business owner (bank loan) to service the business and if something goes wrong in the business the owner is liable to paying off the debt in return for some other assets he might own. But the rules of liability are different in different business structures and all these factors should be looked into before one can make the decision of which business structure is best for your business. As a result, it is always better to consider professional legal advice in this matter as a professional will help you decide better that which structure would be the most appropriate one for you.

Also a professional will see that you have correctly filled out all the required legal documentation required for the chosen business structure. Incorrectly filled documentation or incomplete documentation will only delay your process of establishing your business and will just waste valuable time which might have been spent running on the business and we all know that in the business world time is money.

Types of Business Structures

- Sole Trader: The best business structure to choose if you have troubles taking orders from someone else or if you do not need that many employees to run the business. It is not ideal for high risk business's as in these business's the chances of failure are higher than other business's and since in this business structure you have an unlimited liability, if anything were to go wrong you would have to pay all the debts off using other assets you might have. Also you will be paying self-employment tax on your income.

- Partnership: Partnership is collaborating with another person or company where you end up sharing the different costs, responsibilities and income of the business. No partnership is the same and it comes down do the partnership terms that you agree on with your partner(s). And it is on the basis of these terms that you invest a certain amount of money and then get a certain amount of share from the profits. General partnership is when all partners are responsible for business debts while limited partnership is when each partner is only liable to the extent of their investment amount.

- Company: It is a legal entity that is different from its shareholders and owners. It is the most complex business structure and hence requires a lot more paper work than any other business structure. Also the administrative fees tend to be higher for a company. It is because of all these factors that corporations are better for larger, established businesses that have several employees.

- Franchise: It is an agreement between two separate legally independent identities. The best way to understand a franchise is to think of you opening a McDonald's (a world renowned fast food chain) in your local area. In this case, you would be the franchisee while McDonald's is the franchisor. Once you have opened up your franchise, the franchisor will help you in providing the same products/services as they do in return for a fee that you will pay them. For small business owners, the investment risk and return all are high for owning a franchise.

Choosing a Business Structure

It is vital to remember that before starting a new business, every entrepreneur should very strictly consider his or her limitations in regards to financing and the effort needed to sustain constant development and growth of the business. Each business is unique in its own way and each service it provides also has a differentiating point from other businesses. As a result the obligations, the requirements and the limitations of each business is different and hence one should always keep all of these points in mind when choosing the best business structure for your business. Always remember to choose the business structure that meets your business's current needs and circumstances. Don't worry too much of the long term as if your business needs change in the future you can always change the business structure as well. That is not a problem at all.

Small Businesses

Usually when someone is just starting a business they will start with a small business so right now we will look at which is the most appropriate business structure for a small business. Though there are many types of business structures, the best one for a small business would be being a sole trader or being in a partnership as it is the easiest to set up with minimal paperwork and administrative fees. Though in some situations privately owned companies can also come under small businesses.

Every country has its own specific requirements of business's being categorized as small businesses. For example if we take the number of employees as a measurement for small business, than in Australia, European Union and America small businesses have 15, 50 and 500 employees respectively.

Though the profit margin in small businesses is not much as compared to that of large businesses but many people are happy and content with their small businesses as in most cases they are their own bosses and they can have extra time for their family and for themselves.

Chapter 4. Running a Business

Once you have set up your business and have officially started providing your goods and services, your next goal must be to be able to keep on running your business as smoothly as possible and the best way to do that is to get in touch with your customers, get some feedback from them. Ask them what they like, what they don't and take all of this and then use them to better your business so that it is more beneficial to your customers as happy customers mean a good running business for you. Also from time to time come up with different promotions or special offers so that more and more people are inclined to come to your business. Other than that always try to reduce your own production costs so that you can increase your profits. Lastly, it is important to do good and sensible advertising for your business. After all how will people purchase your goods or services if they don't know about it? So see what things interest your target audience and advertise your business in such a way that it is appealing to your target audience.

Chapter 5. Finding a Business Partner

Though you can always run your business on your own and while there is no harm in that, sometimes it is also great to have a helping hand in the form of a partner, who can help share your burdens and stresses and take some responsibility which means less work load and work pressure on you. Having said that, deciding to have a partner is the easy bit, while finding a partner who clicks with you is the difficult part.

To be able to find a partner you should have a certain criteria in the sense that the person who is your partner should have the same sort of motivation to succeed as you so that you two can constantly push each other in a positive way to reach your potential and go even beyond that. Also you two should have the same missions and goals as to what you want to do with the business and where you want to take it, as there is no point finding a business partner if half the time you will be disagreeing over how to run the business.

Other than that it is also important that you and your partner have a balance. Meaning that he can make up for your weaknesses and you can for his, so that wherever one person is lacking the other can make up for it. In this way when you are running your business, the chances of failure due to your individual weaknesses will be cancelled out by your partner's skills and strengths. Lastly, this is something you would already know but it is still important to mention that you should find an honest and sincere person to be your partner and who has some sort of experience already. Not only that but he should be dedicated and committed to making the business work just like you and wherever you fall short he should be willing to stand by you.

Chapter 6. Investing in a Startup

Investing in a start up is a great experience as it is always satisfying to know that you are helping someone stand on their two feet. Not only that but by investing in a startup, you will be helping to create jobs and also helping in capital formation and these are two important factors for growth for any economy. But these are just personal rewards and apart from these there is also a financial reward in the form of returns from your business which can be up to 5 times to even a 100 times. But before you can invest in any startup it is vital that you do your homework and background checks to see whether the startup you are thinking of investing in, is it really worthwhile.

Always remember to invest in something you know or are familiar with as this helps you to reduce your risks, as you already understand the market in which the startup will operate in. Also do research of the market you are about to enter in terms of your competitors as to who they are and what they do. Run a comparative analysis to see how your business is better than theirs. Another way to reduce your risks are by diversifying your investments, don't use all of your money to invest in one start up, diversify so incase one fails you have others to fall back on.

It is also essential that you look at the founders of the business and make a good check on their background to see whether they are hardworking and committed individuals who will make good use of your money. But that doesn't mean you don't ask them what they will do with that. It is a good thing to ask them how they are going to spend your money, as this will also give you an insight as to how their mind works. Lastly, always review all the legal documents and any other required paperwork before signing it and investing in the startup so you know what you are getting yourself into.

Conclusion

Starting a business may seem daunting at first and never the less it does require lots of hard work, determination and motivation to start it and keep it running. But if you have the mind frame for it and are willing to put in the effort you can make it work. The key is just to break everything down into small tasks and arrange them in a chronological order so you know what has to be done when and you can start doing those tasks one by one. Always have a clear sense of what you want to do and then decide on how you will go about it and whether your current strategies and products are up to your customers satisfaction. And before you know it you will have your own startup business.

If you don't want to take on the entire burden then you can always find a partner with who you can set up your business and in this way your responsibilities will be shared and the partner will also help you in the initial investment. A good business partner can do wonders for your business. Always do all your research and homework before choosing your partner, or your business structure, as these are the most important decisions you will make in regards to your business. Lastly, we always recommend professional help, as professionals will do a great job of explaining all the legalities surrounding the setting up of any business and how it would affect your business. Not only that but they will be able to answer any questions which you may have and their help in filling out the required documentation properly will definitely help you save valuable time.

I want to personally thank you for reading my book. I hope you found information in this book useful and I would be very grateful if you could leave your honest review about this book. I certainly want to thank you in advance for doing this.

www.ingramcontent.com/pod-product-compliance
Lightning Source LLC
Chambersburg PA
CBHW061703050726

47598CB00004B/1644